AN ARTIST'S VISION

Paintings, Drawings and Text by

SUE COLEMAN

The time is near.
The time will come,
When all must join
And think as one.

To protect the land,
The sky and sea
From the greed and grip
Of humanity.

Listen to the totem's sigh.
Listen to the eagle's cry.

An Eagle's Cry

AN
ARTIST'S
VISION

SUE
COLEMAN

Cobwebs of the mind collect
Too soon you find,
All thoughts confined
Within a web of trivialities.

To my husband John Daniel,
for his unwavering support,
encouragement, and patience,
and to my family for being there.

A BEAVER FRONTAL POLE

Acknowledgements

I would like to thank all those who have encouraged me financially or otherwise, and who gave me the support I needed to bring an idea to fruition. In particular, thanks go to the following people: my parents, Mr. and Mrs. Robert Knott; M. Morgan Warren, a very good friend; Ken Budd of SummerWild Productions; Bill McAllum, for the use of his very extensive library; Elaine Jones; Alex Green; Trevor Mills; Bob Faulkner and the staff at Agency Press; the staff at Zenith Graphics and VanType; the native people who encouraged and explained, especially Victor Newman, Douglas Wilson, Tim Paul, Roy Vickers, Bill Reid, John Cennamy, Louis Maynard, and the many others I have met in my travels; Myron Arnt and the staff of Island Art.

Table of Contents

Foreword

In these days of oil spills and acid rain, wildlife art is more popular than ever before. The public consciousness—and conscience—is very strong and we seem to be hanging on our walls images, reminders, of what we are in danger of losing through overcrowding and technology: nature in all her beauty and abundance. However, that which appears fresh and unspoiled in reality can become cliched and stale when rendered in paint, unless the artist makes a totally original statement. I believe Sue Coleman has accomplished this with her fortuitous marriage of traditional British watercolourist realism and west coast native concepts.

One autumn morning in 1988 I had an appointment to meet Sue at the offices of a local printing company in town. Uncharacteristically, my friend was several minutes late but finally arrived looking tired but triumphant. ''I was up till 2:00 this morning finishing my hawk—what do you think of him—looks pretty good for a first attempt, doesn't it?'' she said and, much to the amazement of myself and the press staff, produced with a flourish a stuffed and mounted immature Cooper's hawk, its beak wide open as if screeching in defiance.

I have related this small incident because it tells a lot about Sue and her success: she responds to life in general and to new adventures and challenges in particular with great gusto and tenacity. In the case of the hawk, which a neighbour found dead by their chicken run and had brought for her to paint, she created a new hobby for herself, taxidermy, and stayed up half the night to learn the process because she found it so fascinating. In the case of the West Coast Interpretive Prints, she worked on an idea with no real guidance or sponsorship until her belief in her abilities brought the project to fruition. Many would have paused there, relaxed a little and enjoyed the rewards of popularity, but Sue immediately went to work to create a second unique concept, the ''Power'' series, which proved to be equally as successful as the first. She has, moreover, interspersed both series with other prints which, while not relating directly to a West Coast theme, exhibit in themselves an unusual and often humorous approach to the wildlife genre: a couple of young racoons eyeing some succulent salmon while doing a balancing act on a log; a pair of fuzzy young great horned owls, timorously surveying the great domain beyond their nest. These images anthropomorphize to a degree, but for a purpose: many of the qualities we humans claim to be ours exclusively belong to the beasts and birds, the racoons and the owls of this world, as well. We are not so far removed from them.

In her art Sue attempts to illustrate a fundamental truth: we are not isolated or unique but are part of a greater whole (one which the native people of the West Coast understand and express through their mythology), a living planet which is rich, diverse, and deserving of all our respect.

M. Morgan Warren

M. Morgan Warren
Brentwood Bay, B.C. March 2, 1989

11

Introduction

My whole family considers me a little crazy, but there's something about being "a little crazy" that allows an artist to bend a few rules. It gives one the courage to break new ground and tear down barriers set up by critics in society.

Many times I have been asked what inspired me to translate the art of the Pacific Northwest. An artist is continuously striving to find new ways to express him or herself and the idea sprang from that searching. The year 1980-81 was a particularly difficult one. My husband's vocation, the building trade, was in a slump. I was to give birth to our second child—badly timed given our financial circumstances but a great joy after having waited twelve years since my son's birth.

I had recently discovered the challenge of watercolours after years of working in oils and pen and ink. After spending a weekend at a local show, displaying my watercolours next to the work of Victor Norman, a native carver from Sooke, I had a strong desire to explore native art. At the same time, I was aware that as a non-native, my representations of native art would have little, if any, value. Another passion of mine was wildlife art, and numerous artists had already established themselves in that field. Now I was haunted with native designs.

The two interests came together on the way home from that Sooke show.

I ran my idea by my best critic, my husband Dan. He looked totally blank. Floating images? Myth mixed with realism? Translations? "Put it on paper, Sue," he said. "I can't possibly see inside that crazy head of yours."

It was a wild idea but I really enjoyed blending the two art forms, quickly realizing how essential balance and form are to the design of native art. After completing four pieces I began to think that I had something unusual enough to warrant publication. However, I had some major hurdles to overcome: I was self-taught in this field; I had no records of gallery shows or exhibits; there was no work in the marketplace with which to compare these pieces; and, probably most important to a publisher and business man, I had no proof of past sales. In 1981 and 1982 I approached three major publishers; all were unwilling to take a risk on a ''nobody.'' Without funds to self-publish, it seemed I had come to a standstill in getting my designs to the public.

In September of '82 I put the work on display at a small show in conjunction with another artist and friend, Derek Wynn. The reaction of viewers in the first few hours convinced me to take the plunge; I put ''Not for Sale'' signs on the designs, put together an order sheet and started taking names for limited edition prints of *The Seal*. By the end of the show I had enough orders to pay for the cost of that first print. Over half those orders wanted subsequent prints in the series as soon as they were released, and within six months I had released three prints and had well over 100 steady collectors.

In the succeeding years, public demand and my own curiosity led me to spend many hours in the Provincial Archives in Victoria and to pore over as many books as I could find in libraries and bookstores, searching for more information on the legends of the Pacific Northwest. I travelled to Alaska several times, which brought me into contact with the native people there, and I began to collect their legends and stories. Listening has become as important as seeing; the true culture cannot be seen with the eye alone, it must be felt.

This book is an accumulation of eight years of research and travel, and tells a little of my experiences during that time. I certainly never realized eight years ago what a gift that idea was to become or where it would lead me. I can never be really sure where the idea came from, but I never cease to be thankful.

Sue Coleman

The Seal

The Seal

Last summer in Waddington Channel, an arm off Desolation Sound, I was out in a small boat and noticed a seal on a flat rock close to a cliff. When we circled around, we saw a small silvery mass uncurl and turn a little black head towards us. The afterbirth was still visible on the rocks. The female rolled on her side and raised a flipper. It was a warning, and knowing that possible abandonment might be the outcome, we ventured no further. Unfortunately, I hadn't taken my camera, but the memory will remain fixed in my mind forever.

The seal was extremely important to the Indians of the West Coast. They preserved the meat for winter, rendered the oil, and used the inflated skins for whaling floats. Sealskin pants kept the hunters dry and warm when they went out in their canoes.

Tsimshian legend records a self-propelled, double-headed canoe that had an open mouth at each end. All that crossed its bow or stern would be eaten. When it was put in the water and fed seals, it went very fast; the more seals it was fed, the faster it went. Some say it creaked very ominously when it got hungry.

According to a legend from Cowichan, on Vancouver Island, there once lived ten very handsome brothers that were famous for their skill at hunting seals. They used to boast of their skills and claimed the seal hunting area for their own. In the area lived another family of only five brothers that were very jealous and tried many times to hunt the seal also, only to be fought off by the ten seal hunters. Finally they sought the advice of the wise man who, for the price of one canoe, blankets, and their pretty young cousin, made a seal out of cedar. Using plants and herbs, they brought it to life and instructed the seal to allow itself to be speared by the ten brothers. When they chased it, the seal was to lead them away. This it did, and the brothers were not seen again for many years. By that time they had learned not to be so boastful and greedy.

Rarely regarded as a guardian spirit, the seal gives swimming and fishing skills, and is a symbol of wealth.

The Bear

The Bear

My one encounter with a bear out of captivity was enough for me. Summers ago, touring in the Rockies with my parents, who were on holiday from England, we happened upon a bear browsing alongside the highway. Typical of many tourists, we stopped and I leaned over the top of the car to aim my camera. We had all forgotten our six-month-old pup, who promptly shot out of the car. On scenting the dog, the bear's atitude changed from a docile teddy to a raging foam-mouthed fury. As the bear rose up on its hind legs to better assess the enemy, I threw my camera into the car and ran to grab the dog, who was cowering under the front bumper. The pup's courage returned and he shot back through my legs into the car and left me standing in the path of the charging bear. Fortunately it had a bank to navigate, which slowed its stride enough for me to get back into the car. Mother had closed the door in panic and by the time I had reopened the door and gotten in, the bear was across the road so fast he almost went into the ditch on the other side. We were away just as he was skidding into a turn. My father had been sitting in the front seat calmly filming the whole episode as if we had staged it. It was a pity he had forgotten to take the cap off the lens, but I wasn't about to go back for a second take.

"It is said that if a pine needle falls in the forest, the eagle will see it, the deer will hear it, and the bear will catch its scent." (Jeff Rennicke, *Bears of Alaska*.)

The bear was represented in myth as strong, aggressive, and fearless, symbolizing fierceness and supernatural strength. It is distinguished by a massive, powerful muzzle, alert and aggressive eyes, and wide, flaring nostrils. The bear's muzzle is portrayed as short and square, and usually with a protruding tongue, distinguishing it from that of the wolf.

Several Interior Salish-Shuswap legends tell of how Bear affected the seasons and the length of day and night. In one legend Bear got into an argument with Coyote. (The animal varies; Thompson River-area legend refers to Chipmunk; Shuswap, Coyote.) Bear complained that there wasn't enough darkness and Coyote wanted more light. They tried to outdo one another with powerful songs and dancing and eventually they were both tired out, with neither side a winner. They capitulated and divided night and day equally, but Bear wasn't satisfied. "Winter is too short," he complained. "Let winter be as many moons as feathers in the tail of Blue Grouse." Coyote counted 24 feathers, which were too many. "Let the year be as many moons as feathers in Flicker's tail. Since we are equally matched, winter shall be half that and summer the rest." Bear agreed because he thought there were a lot of feathers in a flicker's tail and he was too lazy to count. There were only twelve feathers, but by the time he found out it was too late. Thus Coyote saved the people from living in darkness and from long, cold winters.

Women endowed with this spirit are industrious,
skilled housekeepers, fine cooks, and good mothers.
Men are strong, skilled and daring.

S. J. Coleman

The Loon

The Loon

Less than one-quarter of a mile down the road is our local beach, which looks out across the Strait of Juan de Fuca. It is not as popular as some; the sand is in short supply, it is mostly pebble scattered with logs at the high tide line. But it can be a quiet place to walk the dog or sit and meditate. It was there one day that I saw the loon. I was sure it was a loon—I knew no other bird that swam so low in the water. I watched for over an hour as it drifted with the tide, periodically dipping its head under the floating weed and foam for morsels of food. As the tide came in the bird drifted closer and my identification was confirmed; it was a male loon. Occasionally it glanced in my direction. I was alone on the beach, just as the loon was alone in the water, and he was such a handsome and obviously available bachelor that I found myself talking to him. When finally I rose to leave I thanked him for sharing the afternoon with me. He turned his head and solemnly stared in my direction, then shook himself and, lifting his body into a running flight, left also.

To the people of the west coast of Vancouver Island long ago, the call of the loon was an eerie sound. The loon was said to have enjoyed scaring those trapped in the fog that often rolled in during the summer months. Because of its speckled plumage, it was given an apt but unflattering name meaning "maggots on the back."

The Dene tell of how the loon got her necklace. A blind man was sad because his wife had been unfaithful, and he was crying by the lake. A loon came to him and asked him why he cried so, to which the man replied, "Alas, I am blind and my wife has left me." Then the loon told the man to sit on her back and bury his face in her neck. He did so and the loon plunged into the lake. When they surfaced he could almost see, and she dove again, and then he could see so well that he gave the loon his most valued possession—his necklace of dentalium shells. He threw it to the loon and it settled around her neck. Next he took a few more shells from the bottom of his quiver and threw them to the loon. The shells settled on her back, and that is how the loon got her marks.

A Tlingit story describes how long, long ago it became very dark, and the people could not find their way. Then they heard a loon calling and they followed the sound until they found the bird, which swam in front of their canoes and led them to daylight. Since that time, the loon has been a special emblem, or crest, for the descendants of those people.

Another legend tells of how some women were doing their washing by the lake when the children playing nearby splashed mud on the clean clothes. The women became very angry, and the frightened children ran into the lake, never to return. The mournful cry of the loon reminds the women of their lost children and that they should always be tolerant.

Women with this spirit achieve skill in weaving and sewing. Men are endowed with great fishing skills.

MORTUARY POLE
NINSTINTS

The Killer Whale

The Killer Whale

The west coast of Vancouver Island is a fisherman's paradise. Cod, salmon and halibut abound, and where there are fish, the predators follow. Seals are so common to the coast that they don't cause any great fluctuation in the everyday meanderings of the fish, but when a pod of whales comes through, there's not a fish to be found. Most weekends my husband and I enjoy going out in the boat; I usually steer while he throws a couple of lines in the water. We're not serious fishermen (at least, not serious enough to be out on the water much before 10:00 A.M., so we usually miss the early bite), but we rarely get skunked and usually come home with something—unless the killer whales get there first, that is. Killer whales frequent the coast, especially during the summer months. At the first sighting, most fishermen reel in and head for the marina, but not us. I dive below into the cabin and grab my camera and we follow the pods, watching and enjoying these huge mammals as they leap and play, reveling in their environment. The thrill of having killer whales surface alongside our boat or watching a female with her calf is better than catching a salmon any day.

According to Tlingit legend, the first killer whale, or blackfish, was created by a successful young hunter who lived in the village of his brothers-in-law. The elder brother-in-law was jealous, and one day he left the young hunter behind on an island beach. The youngest brother-in-law tried to return to help the hunter, but the other brothers wouldn't let him. Eventually, with the help of the seagulls and sea lions, the young man was able to return home safely. To get revenge on his brothers-in-law, he set about carving eight blackfish. First he carved them out of spruce, but they wouldn't come to life. The next day he tried again in red cedar, then hemlock, and finally, yellow cedar. Each time he painted them carefully and every morning sang them his most powerful song. Finally the blackfish carved of yellow cedar came to life and jumped into the sea, swam about and brought fish for him. Then the hunter saw his in-laws far out at sea. He told the blackfish to overturn the canoe and only save the youngest brother-in-law, the one who had tried to help him. This the blackfish did, but after they had saved the youngest brother-in-law, the young hunter told the blackfish that he had made them only to get revenge on his brothers-in-law, and that they were never again to harm human beings. Instead they were to help them if ever humans were in trouble. Then the blackfish swam out to sea, the first blackfish in the world.

*The killer whale, or orca, confers skill
in hunting seal and water birds and also in
the fishing of salmon or halibut.*

The Beaver

COPPER RIVER ALASKA.

The Beaver

Out on the glacial flats of the Copper River the mountains tower green and stark in the distance and in between the muskeg, the swampy pools are dark green. It was here in Alaska that I saw my first beaver lodge. I sat for a long time hoping to see the beaver before I realized the nearby highway had caused the lodge to be abandoned. It was late summer and the mound of sticks stood out among the lime-green swamp grass and red and orange muskeg. It was a stark contrast to the highway's verge, scattered with discarded beer cans and bottles, the empty lodge a monument to the losing battle of nature against the encroaching works of mankind. I've seen many other lodges and dams since, as well as beavers working them, but none remain so vividly etched in my mind as this lodge—abandoned under the pressure of civilization.

The beaver, easily recognized by large incisors and a cross-hatched tail, is not generally elaborated on as a character in myth, but it appears frequently in carving—possibly because of its distinctive form. Tsimshian legends tell of the origin of the beaver. A brown-haired woman dammed up a small stream to make a pool for bathing, and when she swam, her leather apron made a slapping sound on the water. The pool got larger and the husband of the woman became very annoyed, because she was spending more and more of her time there. Then the pool became a lake and one day the husband was so angry that his wife refused to leave the water. That was how she became the first beaver; her brown hair spread over all her body and her flapping apron became her tail.

The Bella Coola woman expecting a child was very careful not to walk on a beaver's dam, or dip her head into a beaver pond. If she did, the birth of the child would be blocked in the same way a beaver dams a stream.

Beaver figures appear prominently among the crests of Eagle phratry Tsimshian as well as Haida. Beaver is a kindly creature credited with bringing warmth to the shivering mortals along the Fraser River. With the help of Eagle, Beaver stole fire from a faraway people, and the first house in the world was built by the father of all the beavers.

There is also a story from the Interior of a boy that mistakenly set his traps on the sun's path. When there was no sun that day the people became anxious and set out to find the sun. They found him trapped fast in the snare but it was so hot they were all burned in trying to free the sun. Then Beaver tried; his teeth were so sharp he managed to cut quickly through the bindings. But the sun was so hot it burned Beaver's teeth and they remain brown to this day.

This spirit represents "medicine power" and the ability to change snow into rain or mist by chanting.

The Eagle

SOOKE BASIN

The Eagle

To watch the eagles circling high in the sky over the coastal islands of British Columbia gives me a marvelous feeling of freedom. Along the shoreline, the startling splash of white against the surrounding green enables the avid bird watcher to quickly spot the proud head as it keeps a constant watch from its craggy post. Observing the calm grace with which it circles looking for prey, seeing the speed with which it swoops and plucks a salmon fromn the water, one can understand why the Indian ancestors chose this bird as one of their most powerful crests.

An Alaskan story tells of a pair of giant eagles, so big they caught whales to feed to their young. One day one of the eagles carried off a young woman whose husband was a great hunter. The hunter climbed up to the nest in a dead volcano and killed both the giant eagles. After that there were no more giant eagles, but eagles still possess the magic and power of their giant forebears, which is why their down and feathers are so valued.

To the natives of the Pacific Northwest, the eagle's down was a symbol of peace and friendship and was sprinkled before visiting guests. Eagle feathers were also used on many other ceremonial occasions.

One of the Tlingit legends depicting the eagle's generosity tells of a very unlucky fisherman who caught so little he had to be given fish by others. One morning when he was very hungry, he heard a voice calling him. On looking around, he saw an eagle. The eagle transformed himself into a human and invited the man to follow. He was taken to a high house and fed fish and game. The fisherman was so well treated there that he stayed and married an eagle woman. In time he became a great fisherman, but what he thought was his spear was actually talons, as he had become an eagle. The rest of his family were equally as poor as he had been, so he left fish for them to find. Through her dreams, his mother knew where to go for the fish and also knew that it was her son that was leaving the fish for the family. One day she spotted him and then she saw that he had turned into an eagle. To honour their eagle benefactor, the family took the eagle for their crest.

In Sitka there are on display four poles from the native dwelling called "Eagle Nest House" that may be over 200 years old. Their design also tells of the eagle's generosity. Once, a long time ago, a young girl and her grandmother were the only survivors of a terrible sickness that destroyed the rest of the clan. They were alone and very hungry when a young eagle found them and brought them fish from the sea. The eagle came to believe the young girl was its mother. The girl survived, eventually married, and had children, insuring the survival of the clan.

The eagle endows the favoured person
with penetrating eyesight, exceptional hearing,
and skill as a hunter of all game.

The Raven

The Raven

Raven is the Transformer, the Trickster. He is the most powerful of all the creatures, not in strength but in his intelligence and quick, unexpected actions. He loves to woo, cheat, and steal but it is usually to the benefit of man. Raven is the key performer in a great many of the coastal legends. Without him and his tricks the world would be a very different place.

Among the native people of the Pacific Northwest, there were many different theories on creation, most of them centring on Raven. A Tlingit legend tells how a brother and sister were the only people on the earth. The brother was very possessive of his sister, but the sister was very lonely. One day she decided to end it all. Noticing a beautiful pebble the shape of an egg in a tidal pool, she swallowed it, thinking it would kill her. After awhile she realised she was going to have a child. The child was Raven. Raven grew quickly, and his mother, fearing her brother might harm him, asked Crane to raise the child. The boy grew up strong and hardy and Crane sent him back to his mother. Thereupon his uncle immediately set out to kill Raven by felling a tree on him, but as Raven was born from stone, he came to no harm. Raven outwitted his uncle many times until one day the uncle called on the tides to rise up. The tides rose and Raven found he could do nothing, so he killed a bird, put on the feathers, and flew up into the sky to escape the rising waters. He stayed at the house of the sun and after some time returned to earth. After flying for many days he eventually found a bit of land, where he waited for the water to recede.

The Haida also have a legend concerning a great flood, and here the story of Raven is continued from the Haida. For many months only the peak of the highest mountain was visible above the raging seas. There sat Raven, wet, bored and hungry. At last the waters receded and finally a strip of beach was exposed. It was covered with seafood. There was so much food all Raven could do was eat, and he gorged himself. At last he couldn't eat another bite and he started to walk the beach, screeching to alleviate his frustration and boredom. Hearing an unusual sound, he looked around but all he could see was an old clam shell half-buried in the sand. He looked closer and saw it was full of wriggling, terrified little creatures, all trying to hide from him. Maybe if Raven hadn't been so full, the world would now be a different place, but as Raven was no longer hungry he decided these creatures might offer him some entertainment. Using his most seductive voice he told the creatures of the world awaiting them, of the big houses they could build and the canoes that would take them on the seas, of the salmon run that came every year to the rivers. He told them of the whales, porpoises, seals, and otters. Finally the strange people came out. They had shiny black hair like Raven but their heads were round and they had no feathers or wings on their bodies. They were the first Haida.

For many years Raven watched the people grow. He amused himself with his new playthings, teaching them all he knew. It was a great game he played with the little people from the clam shell and it lasted many centuries.

The raven has an immortal spirit that likes tidiness; the recipient is a good organizer and can easily kill game.

The Salmon

The Salmon

Fresh salmon on the plate is a luxury we frequently enjoy. Usually my husband is the fisherman, but on one occasion he decided we would try to catch the early bite and he dragged me protesting out on the water at 5:30 A.M. By 9:00 we still hadn't had a good bite. Disgruntled and thoroughly convinced it was all a waste of time, I went below to make coffee while Dan took the wheel.

"If we get a strike it's yours," he called down, in an effort to cheer me up. Seconds later, the line went and I ran to grab the reel. The line continued to run out as I struggled to hold it. It was strenuous work for a person looking for a lazy weekend, and it was an exhausting twenty minutes before I had the fish alongside. It was a big salmon, weighing in at eighteen and a half pounds, and Dan said it was typical that I should have the rod only five minutes before snagging the biggest catch of the year. As far as I was concerned it was my last; fishing is just too much work.

The five species of salmon were important to the native people of the Pacific Northwest coast, and many stories tell how Raven or his counterpart brought the salmon to the rivers, sea, and lakes.

There was a general belief that salmon were a race of supernatural beings who dwelt in a great house under the sea. There they went about their lives in human form until the salmon run, when they assumed the form of a fish as a type of sacrifice. Once dead, the fish spirit could return to its house under the sea if the bones of the fish were returned to the water. Then the being resumed its human form with no discomfort and would return again the next season. The natives took great pains not to offend their benefactors, returning all the bones to the sea, leaving none on dry land in case the salmon should be short an arm or leg. All the coastal tribes had many regulations concerning the salmon.

Tsimshian legends divide the salmon people into five separate villages, putting spring salmon on the far side of the ocean. The spring salmon people were the first to transform into salmon in the spring, alerting all the other villages to follow. The humpback said he would follow last, and not always regularly, but just now and then. The salmon came to the world of the Tsimshian to fish for their own salmon—the leaves of the cottonwood tree—and while there, their salmon bodies were food in turn for the Tsimshian.

This symbol of fertility also confers immortality and wealth. It also has the power to influence the weather.

The Otter

The Otter

A sign at Pedder Bay Marina reads: BEWARE OF OTTERS, Do not leave fish unattended. One morning I came to know how seriously that warning was meant. I was standing on the wharf with my camera when some local fishermen informed me that if I was interested in getting a look at an otter, I would find one on the next finger. When I arrived I saw no sign of the otter, and assumed I was too late until I noticed an unusual bulge that was moving in the canvas of a nearby boat. Suddenly the bottom corner came up and the otter emerged, tail first. But it was not alone. Struggling and pulling, it finally got its prize out of the boat and onto the dock. It was an eighteen-pound salmon, cleaned and gutted. Before I had time to react, there was a shout from behind me and the unlucky fisherman came running down the dock. He had gone up to the marina for a moment and left his catch in the boat. It was too late; the otter was over the side and into the water. I was so mesmerized by the event that, as on many other occasions, my camera was still hanging uselessly around my neck.

The land otter was dreaded by the Tlingit more than any other creature. It was credited with supernatural powers and had a fondness for stealing people away, depriving them of their reason and turning them into Land Otter Men.

The Gitksan believed that meeting the land otter in person could cause insanity. Kitkatla legend said that otters could go into people and go straight to their brains, then gnaw away so they became mindless. They would begin to act crazy, then get sick and die.

It was commonly believed that the shaman was the only one with strong enough powers to control the otter; he could even use the otter as a spirit helper. The Tsimshian word ''Mawatsxw'' means ''like land otter'' and refers to a person whose actions appear crazy or erratic. The land otter is often referred to as a woman and several mythical accounts portray Otter as a woman who entices a man with acts of pleasure or food.

In the National Museum of Canada there is a mask of Land Otter Woman that resembles a human skull. Unfortunately, the relationship between land otters and the human dead is difficult to establish, although Gitksan sources have said that the land otter people take away the souls of those who have drowned.

Nootka legend tells how the otter got its tail. One day Raven, the Transformer, came upon a young man on the beach sharpening a spear. The young man didn't recognise the Transformer and when questioned, he explained that he was making a spear to kill the Transformer, who was coming soon. In the guise of another youth, the Transformer asked to see the spear. When he was handed the spear, he promptly stuck it on the bottom of the young man and banished him to the water, condemning him to forever drag his spear behind him in the form of a tail.

*The recipients of the otter's spirit
become skilled hunters of seals and good
fishermen, and are destined for wealth.*

Sue Coleman

The Owl

The Owl

Living out in the country brings us into contact with many animals and birds, some quite unexpected. One morning we woke up to a snowy owl that was sitting on the fence post at the bottom of the field. At first we thought it was a huge white cat, but when its head turned and those luminous yellow eyes were focused in our direction, we realized what our visitor really was. The owl didn't stay for long and when it took off, the magnificent white wing span, framed by the dark green of the forest behind, was a marvelous sight.

Another time, when we were clearing the bottom field we were visited by a large barred owl that sat in one of the firs bordering the clearing. It was probably expecting our activities to scare up an easy supper. That owl must nest fairly close, because a year later my parents were clearing ground next door for their bungalow, when I spotted the barred owl again, sitting in the crook of a maple tree, studiously watching our activities.

The Tlingit tell a story of great courage, the story of fire. Raven was flying around his lands and congratulating himself on a job well done when he suddenly realized that he had forgotten to give man fire. It had to be brought down from Fire Mountain and Raven immediately set about preparing some boughs of pitch to hold the fire. While he was working he considered the problems of carrying the fire, and he decided to give the job to Owl. Now, although Raven was a generous bird, he was secretly jealous of Owl's beautiful long bill, a bill even longer than his own, and Raven saw the fire as a way of shortening it.

Owl practiced for the long flight, and at last she set out. When she arrived, the heat of the mountain was so great that it singed some of her wing feathers as she was lighting her bough of pitch. The flight back took much longer because of Owl's shortened wings, and soon fire was burning her bill. She badly wanted to douse the branch but she persevered and soon Raven spotted her and flew up to give encouragement. Raven was so excited as Owl neared the tree of pitch that, in an effort to speed things up, he grabbed Owl by the wings and pushed her face-first into the tree, which burst into flame, disfiguring Owl completely.

Naturally Owl became a great hero, but at a high price. She and her descendants could no longer make great flights; her face was flattened; she had a beak instead of a bill; and she had to sleep in the daytime to keep the light out of her eyes. The ashes had speckled her beautiful white coat, and the smoke of the fire had ruined her melodious voice, changing it to a shrill whistle.

The Tsimshian believed that the owl was the shaman's helper and could cause death to the person it flew over. This seemed to be a fairly common belief, as the Kwakiutl also say a person will soon die if he hears the owl call his name.

There are many other myths and legends that involve the owl. The Tlingit of Sitka tell of a selfish woman who refused to share her herring catch with her blind old mother-in-law. She only gave the old woman hot entrails from the fish, which burned her hands. Finally the old woman told her son, who went and got a boatload of fish for his mother and told his wife to go down and get them. Complaining, she went down to the beach, where she started calling for help. She shouted louder and louder, until her voice sounded strange, like a hoot; she had turned into a screech owl. Thereafter, when a young girl was selfish she was reminded of the legend of the screech owl.

Sitka legend also tells of a child that wandered into the woods and eventually became an owl. Even today, walking in those woods, you will hear the owl child crying.

The white owl imparted fishing skills for sturgeon, halibut, or
salmon. The horned and screech owls (guardian spirits of medicine men)
improved hunting skills on land and sea, even in bad weather.

The Heron

The Heron

At the mouth of Pedder Bay there is a large kelp bed. This is a favourite spot for all fishermen, including the best one of all, the heron. The heron will patiently stand for hours, balanced on the floating kelp as easily as land birds perch on branches. Sometimes it stands on one foot or hunches up like an old man. The heron remains motionless for long periods; then suddenly there is a flash of speed and its beak hits the water and emerges with its catch, a contrast to the slow and gangly way the bird takes flight.

When my daughter Joanne is rowing around our moorage there is always a heron that takes exception to someone else near its mud bank, and the raucous cries echo through the mastheads. In late September, when the water table is low, the heron gets its revenge. It flies over the neighbouring country, landing in the local water holes and cleaning them out of marine wildlife. Not even the goldfish ponds are spared.

Among the Squamish Indian folklore there is a story of an old man who had an unusual way of fishing. Instead of spearing the salmon, he merely felt for the fish and rubbed the spear up against them, collecting the slime of their bodies. When he was given a barbed spear point and shown the correct way to fish he became very angry, saying, "Don't tell me how to fish, I prefer the slime to the fish."

Raven the Transformer then took the man's spear and broke it in two. The two halves were set against his legs, the point of the spear was set against his nose, and his neck was stretched like a snake. The old man turned into a heron and flew away.

The Manhousat people have a very different legend for the heron. In this story, Heron had very fat legs, and his size made him very clumsy and it frightened all the fish. Grebe, his wife, continually nagged him for his failures in catching food, so one day he sat down with a mussel shell knife and scraped all the fat from his legs. It was a terrible ordeal but was well rewarded with a great catch of fish. To this day Heron's legs remain slender and he is still an excellent fisherman.

There are many other beliefs surrounding the heron, the origins of which are hard to trace. A Nootka legend tells how Heron was the keeper of the fog or mist, and that he kept it in his kneecaps. In the Tlingit version of Raven's childhood, Heron was chosen to raise Raven. Because Heron stood in the water for long hours, he was considered strong and hardy. This practice was recognized by young men, who stood for long periods in freezing cold coastal waters to strengthen their bodies.

*Those with the spirit of the heron become
well skilled in female crafts, such as spinning
wool, sewing, and drying and smoking salmon.*

Sue Coleman

The Cougar

The Cougar

Almost every year, usually in the late spring, we get a cougar alert. The local schools warn the children not to play too close to the edges of the school fields and mothers pick up those that have to walk any distance. Sometimes the cats elude capture until they are on the outskirts of the city and in the past we have had a cougar almost make it to the Legislative Buildings. They are usually young cats that have come down out of the Sooke hills and have turned south into civilization instead of north. The big cats need a circle of about nine miles and in that circle there will be enough venison, and grazing ground for the venison, to keep the cougar well fed and the deer healthy. The cougar's farming ensures that the balance with nature remains constant.

The cougar, an extremely elusive animal, is also elusive in Indian legend. I did come across a photograph, taken in 1910 by G.T. Emmons, of a carving of a mountain lion (Hawaao) in Kitwanga on the Skeena River. This carving represents the story of an old woman of the clan of Arhteeh. The people had heard that Hawaao was coming up the river, when they heard the crying of an old woman who had gone to the river to get water. They searched for her but found only her ankles. They tracked the lion down and killed it. In its stomach they found haliotis pearl labrets, which they kept as charms.

There are a few references to the cougar in legends, one of which tells of a war between the Sky Chiefs and the animals. In this lengthy legend a great fight broke out, during which Cougar scratched Whale, opening great slits in his side. Whale fled to the depths of the ocean to escape and these slits can be seen from the chin to the breast of humpback and grey whales to this day. Many other animals were trapped in the outcome of the war and are still seen in the heavens in the shapes of the constellations.

An account by William Shelton in his book, *Totem Legends Told by an Indian*, recalls the story of a young Indian called Willapoint Tom, who lived on the slopes of Mt. Rainier. While hunting he came face to face with a two-headed cougar. Willapoint Tom stood his ground and finally the two heads blended into one and the cougar turned and left him. It was a very powerful experience and when Willapoint Tom returned to his home he became a very powerful shaman, living to be over 100 years old.

After doing many hours of research I printed *The Cougar*, and about a month after its publication I had a visit from a local Indian family who were extremely interested in my design. They were impressed that I had managed to depict the cougar so well with the limited information I had. Eventually it was revealed that the cougar was taboo. In legend, members of the tribe that had the cougar as their totem were very powerful medicine men. Any mistreatment or use of the cougar could be an invitation for these people to take revenge. They were nomadic people, so when they did strike they could never be found afterwards. They were also known as the silent ones, or the invisible people. The extent of this belief is hard to confirm, as every native Indian I have spoken to, even as far north as Ketchikan, Alaska (Tlikit), has refused to discuss the cougar, except to say, "We don't like cougar."

The cougar imparts "strong medicine power" and greater than average skill in fishing, hunting, tracking, and stalking.

Sue Coleman

The Power of the Wolf

The Power of the Wolf

On one of my trips to Alaska I had the opportunity to catch a ride with a pilot doing a mail run down the coast to the small fishing outposts. Knowing I was looking for wildlife, my pilot performed several elaborate turns and steep climbs looking for goat, bear, and moose. During a wavehopping run along a flat strip of beach I saw a wolf loping along the shoreline. It was the last place I expected to see a timber wolf, but as he was alone it was probably a young wolf using the shoreline to circumnavigate another wolf's established territory.

"Would you like to circle?" asked my pilot.

"No," I said, "leave him be." The picture of that lone wolf on that wide expanse of lonely beach, miles from anywhere, going undeterred about his business, will remain forever fixed in my memory.

The wolf was regarded by native Indian cultures as having very special spirit powers, particularly for hunting. The Interior Salish tell of how Wolf helped a weak young man by giving him magic arrows that were sure to kill any deer they hit; no matter in what direction he fired, the arrow would find a deer. These arrows saved the young man's family from starvation. In return for Wolf's generosity, the young man shared his wealth and good fortune with the whole tribe, although the tribe had previously shunned him.

A Gitksan myth tells of a wolf that appeared in a village one day. On trying to feed the wolf, the villagers found that it had a bone stuck in its throat, which they removed. The wolf left soon after, but it never forgot the kindness. When a snowfall caused famine in the village, the wolf returned and led the people to several caribou which it had killed for them.

Another story comes from the Inuit, and explains the hunting behavior of the wolf. A poor woman had many children and when her husband died, she couldn't find them enough food to eat. They were always hungry, lean and gaunt. They changed into wolves and are still wandering the land, in search of food to satisfy their hunger.

Kwakiutl mythology ranks the wolf first among all the animals. In myth, Wolf was the first to initiate young humans into the winter dance ceremony. Many of the stories about the wolf involve the deer, the wolf's natural prey. Several legends tell how wolves came to prey on deer, each tribe adding its own embellishments to the story.

One story tells how, long ago, Deer was quite fat. Deer was never challenged by Wolf because he thought Deer must be a very successful hunter to always be so well fed. But Deer kept a food supply in appendages hanging from under his chin and when Raven tricked him and stole this valuable food supply, Deer slowly lost weight. The next time Wolf met him, Deer was as lean as we see him today. Wolf was shocked at the appearance of his neighbour and stared in amazement. Deer began to feel nervous at Wolf's reaction but decided to bluff it out; he opened his mouth and laughed. Then Wolf was even more shocked—he hadn't realised what small teeth Deer had. It was Deer's undoing, and ever since then, deer have been prey to wolves.

In some legends the role is reversed, and Deer manages to outwit Wolf. A Manhousat story tells how Deer was the slave of Wolf, and one of his duties was to sharpen the knives. He hid one under his arm, claiming that it had broken as he was sharpening it. Later, when everyone was asleep, he used it to cut off the Wolf Chief's head and escape in a canoe.

Another legend, from the Nootka, tells of a supernatural white wolf that transformed itself into a killer whale, giving killer whales their white markings and the habit of travelling in groups, as wolves do.

The wolf bestows a happy, helpful spirit with highly developed senses. Men become fine hunters with skill in woodcraft; women are endowed with skill in weaving and mat-making.

The Power of the Eagle

The Power of the Eagle

The eagle, symbolizing authority and power, is a familiar crest of the Pacific Northwest coast tribes. The eagle is usually represented as a kindly, honest figure, almost opposite to Raven. Eagle is one of the two main Haida crests, resulting in powerful portrayals of the bird, painted and carved on many different museum items. Many families on the coast still have the right to use the eagle crest.

From the Tlingit comes an eagle legend that is localized near Port Simpson, B.C. The story was probably acquired from the Tsimshian through intermarriage.

There lived in a village a young man that did nothing towards feeding his family. Instead he fed all his catches to the eagles. His relatives got very annoyed and when winter came, they refused to give the young man any food from the winter stores. He got very hungry and only his uncle's old wife felt sorry for him and secretly left him food when no one was looking. In the spring, when the tribe moved to the summer fishing grounds, no one would take the boy and the old woman who had fed him. Going to bed hungry that night, the boy awoke from a troubled sleep thinking he heard screeching eagles. When he went down to the shore he found fish left on the rocks. Each day, when he heard an eagle call, he would find many kinds of food left on the reef. All these he and the old woman stored away in cedar boxes. In the meantime the rest of the village was starving because the summer salmon run had not come. The chief began to feel guilty about the young man and sent a slave and his wife to see if the boy was still alive. They returned and told the chief how much food the young man had, and the chief decided to return. When he got to the village he handed over all his wealth and belongings in return for food. The young man was then chosen to be chief, and he married and became very wealthy.

Some of the strongest powers the eagle bestowed on those favoured were powerful eyesight and hunting skills. This spirit was highly respected.

The Power of the Bear

The Power of the Bear

Buckwheat and Camas were the names given to two orphaned bear cubs that were Metchosin's best-kept secret for the spring of 1987. The cubs had been abandoned when logging disturbed the mother bear. They were the size of puppies and their eyes hadn't opened yet. When I first saw them they were already three months old and the size of a medium dog. I had my daughter Joanne with me and filmed her playing with them for over an hour.

The second time I visited they had grown much larger. Buckwheat, the male, was the most trusting and adventuresome. He was the first down out of the tree that they always scampered to when an unknown car pulled into the yard. Usually Camas waited to see if anything became of Buck before she joined in any new exploration. Because they had a large wilderness acreage, our neighbours allowed the bears free range. At first they didn't go far from home and food, but the inevitable happened and they were spotted by some unsuspecting hikers. Wildlife officers were called in and now Buckwheat and Camas are down in Skwim, Washington, on a game farm that caters to bears. I painted the poses of the cubs on the poles in The Power of the Bear *from the film that I took of Buckwheat and Camas.*

There are several versions of the Bear Mother myth, which describes how a young woman marries a bear. Some say she was enticed by a young man who was really a bear in human form. Others say that she laughed and made fun of the big clumsy bear and he carried her off. She bore two children who were half-bear and half-human; they were very wild and even when the woman brought her children down to the village, they were so fierce that they had to go back and live with the bears.

Haida legend tells why, until they were recently reintroduced, there were no frogs in the Queen Charlotte Islands. At one time there were many frogs. One day, when the Frog Chief was hopping down a forest trail, he encountered a black bear. The legend varies here; some say the bear tried to step on the hopping creature for fun, another tells how the bear put the little animal in its mouth to see if it was good to eat, and finding it wasn't, spat it out. Frog, fleeing for his life, returned to his village and related his frightening experience. Fearful that the bear might try to seek them out, the frogs decided to leave the islands.

The Tlingit had taboos against eating bear meat. These beliefs were based on the role the bear played in their ancestral stories. The Haida were less stringent, but would only go hunting after long, purifying sweat baths. If a bear was taken, only small portions of the meat would be eaten, out of respect for the animal.

The powerful strength of the bear was greatly sought after as the protégés possessed great endurance and the strength required for hunting large game.

The Power of the Raven

OLD MASSET BEACH

The Power of the Raven

The raven is a very important bird in Indian legend, but it was some time before I had the material to be able to portray it. After several trips around the southern tip of Vancouver Island, looking for good locations to spot ravens, I finally realized that what I had thought were large crows living in the trees behind our house were, in fact, ravens. We didn't have livestock at the time, and so it took several weeks before we could lure the raven close enough to photograph or sketch. We threw all kinds of meaty morsels on our garage roof but the clever raven only came to feed early in the morning and no matter how early I set my alarm clock I always missed the bird. Finally the raven ventured down one evening and I was able to get my sketches. We stopped putting out scraps for the raven to eat, but the bird didn't leave; instead it turned to raiding our garbage cans. We had to build a locker for the cans before the raven finally gave us up as a lost cause. It still circles hopefully at least once on leaving its roost before heading out on its daily flight.

There are many legends that explain why Raven is black. A Bella Coola legend relates that when Raven was being prepared for his trip to earth he was adorned in many colours and was very handsome. But the vain Raven wasn't satisfied; first he wanted his arms changed, then his legs, and so on. Finally Alkuntam, the great Sky Chief, became angry and told his assistants to throw ashes all over Raven. This made Raven black all over and in this form he was sent to earth.

Another legend tells how Owl, in return for the beautiful coat that Raven had given her, tried to make Raven a gift of a white coat. When it came to fitting the coat, vain Raven kept trying to see his reflection and in the fidgeting knocked over the coal oil lamp, staining the garment. This made Owl so angry she flung the rest of the oil over Raven, and that's the way he stayed.

Other stories say Raven got stuck in a smokehole trying to escape from one of his adventures and was blackened by the smoke. Raven also taught the Bella Coola how to make their eulachon nets. When they ran out of fiber, he told them how to draw it from their own intestines; spiders have had this ability ever since. The Dene legend of fire tells how fire was kept by only one old man and how Raven danced till the old man fell asleep and then stole the fire. When he was running away, Raven spilled some of the fire, setting the woods alight. Since then people have always had fire, which remains in the woods. This is why wood burns easily and why fire can be made by rubbing two sticks together.

The raven was a highly valued guardian spirit with almost uncanny powers, which gave hunters the ability to easily find and kill game.

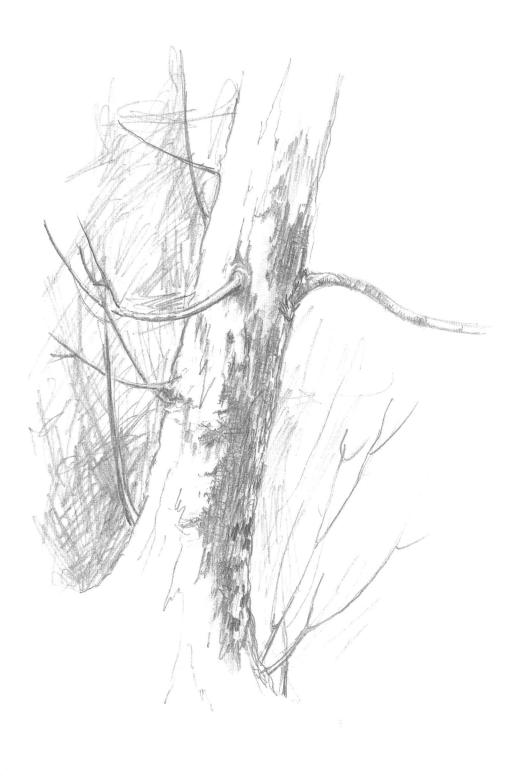

The Wasp

The Wasp

Every summer we take time to check around the eaves of the house for the development of small, cone-shaped paper wasp nests. We have several varieties of wasp; the mud wasp is the worst for the sting, but it seems to be less attracted to fruit or peanut butter sandwiches. With children playing close by, a nest could be a hazard.

Weirs Beach is a mile down the road from home, and on a sunny day in the middle of September the beach is deserted except for its supply of wasps. Here I don't interfere with the wasps that buzz around me as I relax on the beach. If they don't bother me, I don't bother them; there are just a few days of summer left before their lives end naturally.

The figure of the wasp, or bee, as it is known to some native cultures, was intended to amuse during the potlatch. The wasp danced among the spectators and if stung the offended party could be assured of an extra gift during the potlatch for his damages. The Kwakiutl were particularly fond of the wasp interlude, so much so that a whole family would dress as wasps, each with his own mask, including the children. The masks were distinctive. Each nose was covered in spikes or barbs, allowing the wasp to sting more than once.

The hornet and wasp spirit makes its home in the cold north. This gives it strength as a warrior, hunter, and fisherman. The wasp can always gather food easily and endure great hardships during a long hunt or war.

Sue Coleman

*Because its home is in the cold north, this
spirit gives strength to a warrior who is able to
endure hardship during a long hunt or war.*

The Mosquito

The Mosquito

"Indeed men from all countries agree that the musquitoes of B.C. are unmatched for numbers and ferocity."

Dr. Cheadle from his Diary, 1863

The mosquito must be one of the most annoying pests that was ever sent to plague mankind. It is very difficult to see the positive aspects of the insect, which can turn a peaceful evening watching the sunset at the beach into an armed camp, with mosquito coils and sprays forming an ineffective barricade between the watcher and the attackers. Most people are also familiar with the experience of lying awake on a summer night, hearing that annoying drone in the dark and then feeling the tension that builds when it stops.

For the native Indian population along the coast, the mosquito must also have been a problem. Their traditional method of preventing mosquito stings was to coat the skin with rendered deer fat. It was stored in a kelp tube, into which it was poured when molten.

It seems that every tribal group in the Pacific Northwest has a tale to tell of the mosquito and most of the legends are spun around a large cannibal monster, who, through various forms of trickery, is trapped and burned. As in most native Indian legends, there is a twist to the end of the story: the ashes from the fire turn into clouds of mosquitoes.

In the Haida legend a giant spider is burned and when the miniature version, the mosquito, returns, it not only sucks blood but leaves a particle of fiery ash in every bite.

The Kwakiutl legend of Nan-wa-kawie, an ancestor of Chief Wakias of Alert Bay, was carved on the chief's housepole in 1899. This pole is now on display in Stanley Park, Vancouver, where it was moved in 1927. The legend involves a cannibal giant from Forbidden Valley. The lives of four sons of the wise one, Nan-wa-kawie, were at stake and a fire pit was dug and the monster invited to a feast. There he was lulled to sleep and his chair tipped into the pit.

According to Tsimshian legend the monster was a blood-sucking chief with a crystal proboscis. A woman whose child was killed by the monster hid in a tree overhanging a lake, so that her image was reflected in the water. When the monster looked in the lake, he saw her reflection taunting him, making fun of his crystal nose. Thereupon he attacked it, diving into the lake after her reflection. As he came out of the water, the North Wind froze him, enabling the woman to finish the job by throwing him on the fire. To this day, smoke and fire is still feared by the mosquito.

The Tlingit tell of an unusual child born with sharp points on his head. One day, when angered, he killed his own mother and then started killing other villagers. The boy's uncle set a trap for the boy and wounded him with a poison arrow. The boy pleaded for his life, but because he had killed so many people he was put to death. His body was then burned to ashes that were driven about by the wind, resulting in the mosquitoes that torment us to this day.

Mosquitoes have been carved on many masks and ladles. One of the oldest has the proboscis and teeth inlaid with haliotis shell, leather wings fringed with eagle down, and walrus whiskers on the head. It was collected by the Russian explorer Voznesensky in 1840, and is now in a museum in Leningrad.

*Despite its appetite for blood, the mosquito is
symbolic of the soul's immortality; the spirit imparts
the ability to heal the sick if the protege is faithful.*

Sue Coleman

The Frog

The Frog

Scholars tell us that when legends concern frogs, they are often referring to toads. I decided to use a frog in my depiction; we have so many of them in our bottom pond that finding a subject wasn't hard—it was getting it to pose that was difficult. Joanne was a great help, offering her services in catching likely subjects. We had them in all shapes and sizes. I chose to paint a little green tree frog, partly because it was the hardest to catch, but also because of an incident neither of us will forget. In the course of catching the little fellow I decided to get a family picture. I asked Joanne to open her hands slowly near her face and look closely at the frog, and I set the camera and got ready. Slowly Jo opened her hands, but the frog wasn't so slow. It leapt, straight onto Joanne's face, landing squarely on her nose. The registration of shock, then laughter, was some of the best photography I've ever taken; for once I was ready.

Frogs and toads are a popular folk theme throughout the world and occur in many different legends of the Pacific Northwest. The frog's shape readily lends itself to the carving of bowls or mortars and frogs are depicted on many totem poles. The wide toothless mouth and flippered feet confirm the identity.

The legendary figure from the Haida, The Volcano Woman, had a frog-son who was destroyed by thoughtless youths. She is often shown with frogs on her hat and on her cane.

A Tlingit legend records how the frogs spread. A chief's daughter made fun of a frog and was lured into the lake by a frog in human form, whom she eventually married. Her parents, unable to persuade the frog people to release their daughter, dug a ditch and drained the lake, scattering the frogs in all directions. None of the frogs were harmed, as the villagers wanted only the girl, and finally they found her. On returning to the village with her they found she could not eat. She told the people about the frogs and the black mud that they ate. The villagers drained the black mud from her, but when it was all gone she died. The village people learned enough from her that they felt they understood the frogs and the frogs understood them.

A legend from the Athapaskan connects the frog to the mosquito. It is the story of a young man who married the only daughter of a distant chief. He was a good hunter and provided a lot of meat for his new family, and everything went well until one day when he dropped his kill on the way home and it sank into a bog. The family didn't believe him and when he took them to the swamp to prove his story, they found it was full of frogs. The family gathered up the frogs to take home to eat. The hunter thought this was strange, especially as they could only carry one frog each, and he carried forty. He was puzzling over the way they walked when a mouse woman pulled him to one side and told him they were really mosquitoes, and that he would die if he ate their frog meat. The young man left his wife and fled back to his people.

Sue Coleman

The frog is a watchman bringing good fortune
to the people. His spirit is very powerful
and never portrayed in winter dances.

The Hummingbird

The Hummingbird

We have a feeder that we put out each year for the hummingbirds. In the spring, if we're late, the earliest bird will tap on the window with its beak. Once the feeder is up, that early bird seems to exert all its energy in defending the feeder. Eventually it is outnumbered and has to relinquish ground, but not without many bitter squabbles.

The feeder hangs in the family room window and watching the birds feed is hypnotic. A japonica bush beside the feeder is an added attraction in the spring when the flowers bloom. After the nesting season the hummingbirds fly north, but in the fall they return again for a short visit before returning south. By that time the fuchsia flowering on the sundeck gets the attention. When it's time to leave, the birds parade in front of the window and across the top of the fuchsia—a little farewell before heading south.

Sah sin, the hummingbird, is not often seen in Pacific Northwest coast art. However, Ksan member and artist, Robert Sebastion, writes, "Long ago, one of the signals for good luck and good weather to come was the sight of the hummingbird. When hunters prepared for a hunt, they sang Indian songs that would ask the hummingbird to appear, to inspire a successful hunt and healthy game."

A Squamish legend connects the hummingbird to the bee or wasp, who were credited with ripening salmonberries, and it has been recorded that among the crests of certain Wolf phratry on the Upper Skeena River, there is a connection between the hummingbird and the mosquito. Quite by accident, I came across a Haida legend, which also seems to form a connection between these two spirits. The bird in this legend is very descriptive of the hummingbird, particularly the nest description.

Sun had been gambling and on his way down his path, he heard an unusual humming noise. He followed it until he came to a pond, where he saw many nests made of moss. While Sun was looking at the moss hanging from the branches of the tree, a small bird flew out, straight towards him. It made a humming noise and had a very long bill. The outside of the nest was green and Sun thought it was the home of dreaded Mosquito. He took a stick and struck the nest down. When he picked it up he found it was very light. Just as Sun turned, a great cloud of minute mosquitoes rose up like ashes and started to sting Sun for what he had done. He ran very fast over the water and sank down into it. To this day, mosquitoes still hover over the water, looking for the sun.

Small and swift, the hummingbird confers the qualities for being a fast runner and a good warrior with excellent eyesight.

Sue Coleman

The Seagull

Long Beach   Vanc. Isl.

The Seagull

The seagull is the scavenger of beaches worldwide, and the raucous companion of fishermen everywhere, always on the lookout for an easy meal.

We were fishing for salmon off the west coast during the seasonal fall herring spawn one year, and the herring were massing in great balls on the surface. It attracted thousands of gulls from miles around, and their cries were deafening. We had our lines set thirty to forty feet deep and when the rod bent and the line started running, we thought we had a big one; it was certainly putting up a good fight. The thrill was short-lived. As we got clear of the turmoil, we realized we had a young gull on the end of the line. It was the gull's lucky day; the line hadn't broken and it held strong as we reeled it in. When we got the bird on board we discovered the hook well set through its beak—it would have prevented the gull from feeding. It didn't struggle as I gently twisted the hook free. I lifted the bird over the side and threw it up into the sky, where it didn't hesitate to return to the screaming throng of gulls still massing over the water. It didn't look back, oblivious to the uncomfortable end it had just escaped.

From the Salish comes a legend that is repeated in many forms: The Origin of Daylight.

Long ago it was always dark and Kwaietek (Seagull) alone had daylight stored in a box. Raven was determined to share this precious treasure so one day he went down to the beach and collected many sea urchins, ate their contents and then spread the shells at Seagull's door, where he couldn't help but tread on them. Sure enough, because it was dark, Seagull didn't see the shells and stepped on them. The spines sunk deep into his naked feet. When Raven visited later that day, he found Seagull in great pain and offered to help remove the spines. He deliberately fumbled in the dark, causing Seagull so much pain that he cried out. "I'm sorry, but it's so dark I can't see what I'm doing. Open your box so I can see better," said Raven. Seagull did as his brother suggested but Raven still hacked away, pretending to take the spines out. Again Seagull cried out and Raven said, "It's your own fault. I need more light. Here, give me the box." Seagull cautioned him not to open the lid too wide. Raven opened it half way, but slipped and knocked the lid wide open. The daylight flew out and spread itself across the sky so that it could never be captured again, and Seagull to this day has not ceased his plaintive crying.

The Haida have a legend that tells of a powerful grandmother that controlled the tides and kept all the fish in many boxes in her house. Raven, as usual, was very hungry and had asked the grandmother for food and had been refused. Walking down the beach he came across Seagull and Crane. Seagull had just swallowed a dead fish that the grandmother had thrown out. Raven wanted the fish, so he got Crane and Seagull to argue by telling lies in the ears of each bird. Crane became angry and went and kicked Seagull in the stomach, causing him to regurgitate the fish. Raven promptly rubbed his beak in the scales of the fish. Then he went back to the grandmother and taunted her by saying that it was silly to keep fish in her house when there was more fish than she ever had on the beach. At this she became vexed and when the tide came in, she emptied all her fish into the water. Thanks to Seagull and cunning Raven, there are all kinds of fish in the waters today.

The seagull spirit is protective and often rescues stranded fisherman.

The Cormorant

The Cormorant

The black flocks of cormorants interspersed with the white flecks of gulls are a common sight covering the rocks in and around Bentick Island and the Race Passage. Common to the coastal waters of British Columbia, they are frequently spotted drifting with the tide on a log, looking as though they're afraid to get their feet wet and stretching their wings out to dry like Monday's washing. There is always a cormorant standing silent like a sentry on the pillar buoy that marks the entrance to our marina. Used to the steady traffic of boaters, he rarely takes flight and provides an excellent subject for study with the camera or binoculars. The low-level flight of the cormorant as it flies across the waters in front of the boat is very distinct, a streak of black against silver grey.

This Bella Coola legend tells of Raven and Cormorant on a fishing trip. On the trip, Raven didn't do as well as Cormorant (sometimes referred to as Sea Raven), who soon had a mound of fish at his end of the canoe. Cunning Raven then started to admire Cormorant for his phenomenal success, going on to praise his sharp eyes, his fine teeth, his shapely form, and his sweet voice. At first, Cormorant was too busy to listen to such chatter, but after awhile Raven said, ''The only part I can't admire is your tongue. Please stick it out so I can see it.''

The flattered Cormorant stuck out his tongue, and when he did, Raven seized it and cut it off. When Cormorant tried to speak, he only gurgled, and when the two returned to the village, the wily Raven told the villagers that Cormorant had become so sick he hadn't caught any fish and had lost his voice. When Cormorant frantically tried to talk, Raven translated the inarticulate utterances as support for his own lies.

Since then Cormorant's tongue has remained short and he cannot speak like other birds, but can only grunt and gurgle.

This spirit is beneficial to fishermen, imparting skill in spearing salmon.

The Sun

The Sun

Enjoying the ocean as we do, our family has spent most of our winter and summer holidays somewhere on the west coast.

From Alaska to Hawaii, there is little to challenge the Pacific sunset. The speed with which the sun melts into the ocean in Hawaii is rivalled by the multi-coloured clouds of an autumn sky in British Columbia. But the flamboyant sky-blue-pink with fluorescent snow-capped mountains that envelopes Prince William Sound, Alaska, in late May is awe inspiring. The sun wraps even the icy north with a show of warmth and splendour.

The sun is portrayed as a round, humanoid face, usually surrounded by rays of light. A bird beak, often like a hawk's, juts from the faces of the masks, and sometimes copper is used. According to many different accounts, Sun is a gambler.

Sun is the traditional clan totem of the Tsimshians living along the Nass and Skeena rivers and its spirit controlled their destinies. In Sun's house, there was perpetual sunlight, and it was given to mortals for their use by opening and closing great doors in the east and west. The way to Sun's house was well guarded. Bear guarded the sunrise and the sunset was supported by a great post that stopped Sun from falling into the lower world.

In Haida myth, light was originally the exclusive possession of the Chief of the Heavens. The primary act of Raven was the theft of the daylight. In one legend a woman married the Chief Sun and conceived from his rays which struck her every morning through a chink in her house. Light is thus an attribute of divinity and implies power and potency.

A Kootenay legend tells of how the sun and moon came to be chosen. A chief gathered all the village together to decide who would be the sun. First Raven was chosen, but the day proved too dark. Then Chicken Hawk tried but the day was too yellow, like bad weather. When excitable Coyote leapt into the sky for his turn, the day was too hot; even in the shade the children cried because the sun was burning them.

In a nearby village lived a woman with two sons and they decided to go and play in the sky. The elder went first. He came up cool, got warmer as he went higher and came down cool again in the evening. The chief was so pleased that he made him Sun. Not to be outdone, the younger brother was made Moon to give the people light in the nighttime. Coyote was angry and tried to kill Sun with his bow and arrow. His arrows caught fire and set the ground alight and Coyote had a very narrow escape. Never again did Coyote challenge the strength of Sun.

The sun is the spirit centre of the solar system and makes for a brave and strong warrior. But the protege must be fair and just or he will lose his power, be shamed, and die.

The Moon

The Moon

Sometimes I feel sorry for those unfortunate people that must be bound to the city for work or other reasons. They can never freely enjoy the tranquility of the night. Their moon loses its brightness competing with the city lights and the night sounds are lost in the noise of traffic.

The man in the moon, the image of a man trapped on the face of the moon, is conveyed in rhyme to English children at a very early age. To find a similar belief in the legends of the Pacific Northwest is not surprising; there is a great comfort to be shared the world over by looking up at that ageless yellow face. Its reflective light illuminates the whole night sky and the rays slide between the trees and through the window to settle on the pillows of sleeping children everywhere.

Portrayals of the moon vary. Sometimes it is depicted as a serene, handsome young man. At other times, a beak or wing feathers (that is, Raven) are added to the image. In other renditions, the moon is shown with an added crescent form.

The moon crest was used exclusively by four or five Haida chiefs, among whom was the chief of the Skedans. Legend has it that Koong, the Moon, saw Ethlinga, the man, as he set out to pick salal berries. Koong, being displeased with Ethlinga, sent down a magic ray and grabbed Ethlinga, along with his bucket and salal roots, and took him up to the sky, where they have lived ever since. Ethlinga is a friend of T'kul, the spirit of the winds, who from time to time signals Ethlinga to empty his bucket, causing the refreshing rain to fall.

From the Thompson River comes a legend telling how Moon once was an Indian. He would have been as bright as Sun if it wasn't for his sister, Frog. Moon decided to invite all the stars to his house, and it became so crowded that when his sister arrived she couldn't find any place to sit down. She jumped around and landed on Moon's face, where she stuck. The changes that are seen in Moon from night to night are due to Frog's shadow. Whenever it threatens to rain or snow, Moon builds a house around himself—called a halo by humans—and cirrus clouds are the smoke from the pipe he holds in his hand.

Another legend from the Thompson River tells how Sun and Moon were great chiefs who looked after the people. They both shone at the same time, but one day they started arguing. Sun accused Moon of not giving enough of his light so that the people were cold and couldn't see very well. Moon accused Sun of burning the people and blinding them when they looked at him, probably because Sun was ugly and didn't want the people to see his ugly face. This upset Sun so much that they decided to part, Sun shining by day and Moon at night.

The moon's protege is endowed with a medicine spirit with the ability to heal the sick and control the souls of ailing people.

Free Ride

This is one of my favourite paintings for several reasons. One is the subject matter; the recollection of a young loon snuggled on the back of a parent bird evokes a feeling of the security of the family unit and made it a joy to paint. I had had a testing week working with a very small subject, a winter wren. It went badly and as watercolours are unforgiving, I found myself throwing hours of detailed work in the wastepaper basket. I needed to relax, and as I had already painted and studied the loon in the past, I turned to it to relieve my frustration and restore my self-confidence. *Free Ride* was the result.

Loon and Chick   Free Ride

112

© 1987 Sue Coleman

Up Close

Tundra wolves, the villains of the tundra, are usually off-white or light grey in colour, as opposed to the darker coat of the timber wolf to the south. Tundra wolves remain north of the tree line all winter, feeding on caribou, musk ox, squirrels and lemmings. They are huge animals weighing 125 pounds or more, and are long-legged for fast travel and deep-chested for staying power over long distances. With large feet for traction in the snow and a heavy coat for protection against the elements, the tundra wolf is a predator, superbly designed and built for the task.

This is a condensed version of text found in many books describing the wolf, but it only tells part of the story. A must for all concerned with the wildlife of this continent is the book by Farley Mowat, *Never Cry Wolf*, subsequently made into a movie. The portrayal of the wolves' family units and the caring shown by these animals can never be forgotten. As I painted *Up Close*, I was continually reminded of this movie, and I think I was secretly envious that Farley Mowat had gotten as close in reality as I could only get in my imagination.

Howling Wolf

Up Close

Sue Coleman © 1987

Intrepid and Snowtime

An unusual and rather gratifying set of circumstances happened after the completion of *Intrepid*. I had, on loan from the Provincial Museum, a young mounted owl as a model for this painting. It had been part of a large display that had for reasons of portability been broken up. I could only vaguely recall the shape of a horned owl's nest and the museum helper had said that it was a large mass of sticks and small branches, much like the nest of any large bird, such as a raven or an eagle.

When I returned the mounted bird to the museum I took my painting with me to get an opinion on the accuracy of the nest. I was asked if I had seen the newly installed "Birds of Prey" exhibit, and when I said I hadn't, I got a very odd look, and was directed to have a look at it; it would answer my question. My curiousity aroused, I made my way to the exhibit, and there, to my amazement, I found an almost exact duplicate of the nest in my painting. True, there were no fledgelings, only a mature female sitting on the nest, but the positioning of the branches and the supporting tree would make it very hard for me to deny having seen that nest before. Many of us can relate premonitions and insights but few have put it on paper. When it happens to me, as it has on numerous occasions, I don't question it any more; the native people never did.

Sue Coleman © 1988

The Great Bank Robbery

You have to be a city dweller to think racoons are cute. Move to the country, buy yourself a dozen chicks, raise them to maturity, collect a few dozen beautiful brown eggs, then tell me what you think of racoons the day after your coop has been vandalized. We don't have chickens any more but we still have a racoon that patrols the neighbourhood. We call him The Colonel; he seemed to think our chickens were finger-lickin' good. No matter how we barricaded the hens, he devised a way to break in. One night he went through two layers of chicken wire and managed to tear away the wall panel of the coop and escape with two hens, all in such stealth that the hens didn't realize their fate until it was too late. Then their panic brought us running to the scene of destruction, where there was no sign of the offender; although there was enough evidence to convict him for life, it was a clean getaway.

I'm sure that racoons are schemers from birth, plotting, planning and devising devious ways to get their next meal. They are well marked by nature with their black eye masks. In *The Great Bank Robbery* the task might be beyond the abilities of these two bounders, but if they did succeed, no one would begrudge them the victory, it would be well earned.

The Rascals　　*The Great Bank Robbery*

118

Sue Coleman

Sue Coleman

Seal Pup

Sue Coleman — Biography

Born and educated in England, Sue gave up her maiden name, Knott, when she married a Canadian and immigrated to Canada in 1967. She quickly fell in love with her chosen country and settled with her husband Dan on the southwest coast of Vancouver Island to raise a family.

Having received a distinction for her art at Cambridge during her school years, Sue continued to pursue the arts, trying many different mediums and looking for new and exciting challenges. In 1980, she turned to watercolours, a medium that still delights her today, with new challenges in every painting.

A realist and a romantic, Sue was completely overwhelmed by the beauty of Vancouver Island and the Pacific Rim. Her paintings often capture those elusive moments when one is at peace with nature, and the pressing crush of modern civilization can be forgotten. She is a supporter of the B.C. Federation of Wildlife, and her awareness of history and culture, and of the delicate balance of the environment and how it can affect the future, is reflected in her work.

Sue's fascination with the art and history of the Pacific Northwest stems from a general interest in history. She was born in Colchester (Camulodunum), England's oldest recorded town, Queen Boadicea's capital, and the home of Olde King Cole. It was natural to her to explore the local history of B.C. and she was especially attracted to native myths and legends. The visual interpretations of the Pacific Northwest legends came together with such a burst of energy that her first four images were on paper in less than a week. Sue then turned to researching in depth, afraid to present these images to the public in case she had inadvertently misrepresented the legends. It was nearly a year later, 1983, before she was satisfied and released her first print. Two of the initial four paintings were discarded and the subjects repainted.

In the subsequent years Sue has researched over thirty animals represented in the native art of this region, eighteen of which have resulted in artwork that is both distinctive and informative.

Index of Prints

* Sold Out

Native Nations of the
Pacific Northwest

Ninstints, Anthony Island

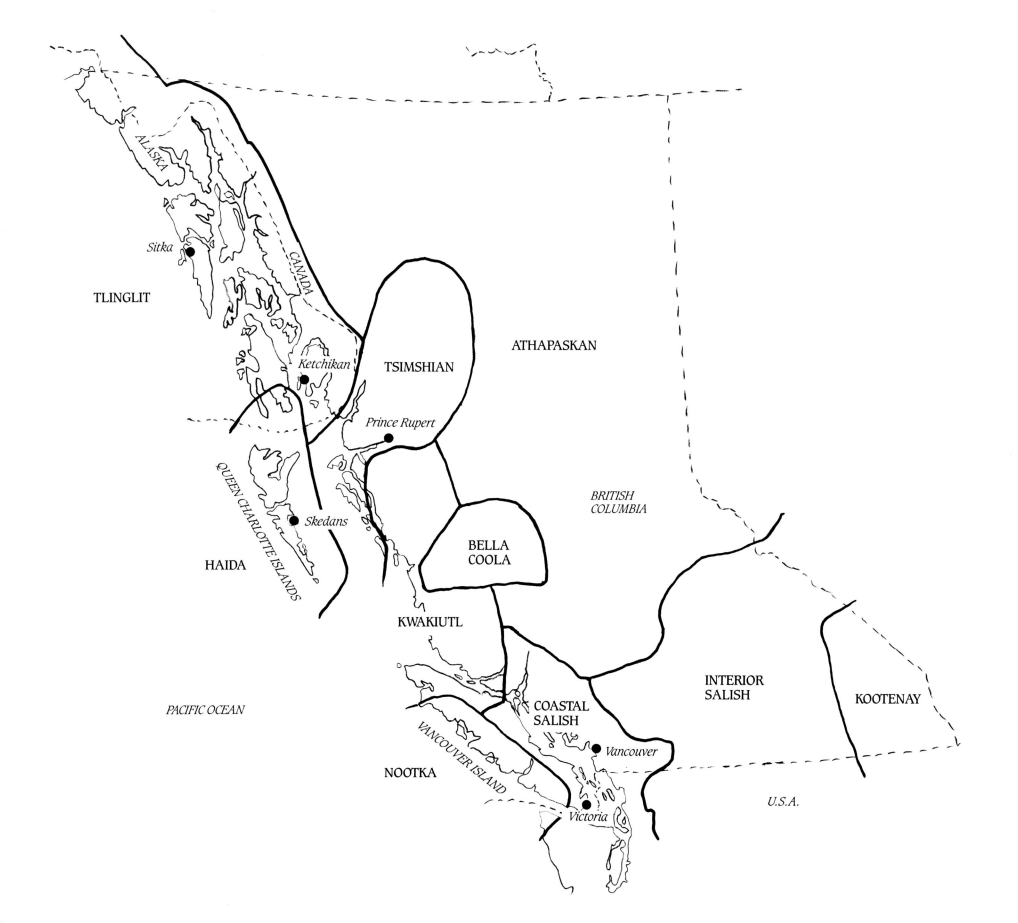

ALASKA

CANADA

Sitka

TLINGLIT

Ketchikan

TSIMSHIAN

ATHAPASKAN

Prince Rupert

QUEEN CHARLOTTE ISLANDS

Skedans

BELLA
COOLA

BRITISH
COLUMBIA

HAIDA

KWAKIUTL

PACIFIC OCEAN

INTERIOR
SALISH

KOOTENAY

COASTAL
SALISH

Vancouver

NOOTKA

VANCOUVER ISLAND

U.S.A.

Victoria

Bibliography

This book is not meant to be a complete overview of the art and myths of the Pacific Northwest, but to give a taste of the variety of themes, and an insight into the past. Much of the material here originates from the writings of the following historians: Marius Barbeau, Franz Boas, Wilson Duff, Alice Ravenhill, John R. Swanton, and James Alexander Teit. Unfortunately, most of their works are contained within the archives and are not easily available for casual reading.

The following books are more readily available from local libraries and bookstores, and contain many of the legends referred to in this book.

Arima, E.Y. *The West Coast (Nootka) People.* Victoria: The British Columbia Museum, 1983.

Belton, Peter. *The Mosquitos of B.C.* Victoria: Museum Handbook #41, 1983.

British Columbia Heritage Series. Series 1, *Our Native People:* Vol. 2, *Coast Salish;* Vol. 3, *Interior Salish;* Vol. 4, *Haida;* Vol. 6, *Tsimshian, Vol. 7, Kwakiutl;* Vol. 8, *Kootenay;* Vol. 9, *Dene;* Vol. 10, *Bella Coola.* Victoria: B.C. Provincial Archives.

Brown, Vinson. *People of the Sea Wind.* New York: Collier, a Div. of Macmillan, 1977.

Drucker, Philip. *Indians of the Northwest Coast.* Washington, D.C.: Bureau of American Ethnology, Smithsonian Institute, 1955.

Ellis, David W., and Shaw, Luke. *Teachings of the Tides, Uses of Marine Invertebrates by the Manhousat People.* Nanaimo, B.C.: Theytus Books, 1981.

Garfield, Viola E., and Forrest, Linn A. *The Wolf and the Raven.* Seattle: University of Washington Press, 1948.

Griffin, George H. *Legends of the Evergreen Coast.* Vancouver: Clarke & Stewart Co., 1934.

Hawthorn, Audrey. *Art of the Kwakiutl Indians.* Vancouver: University of British Columbia Press, 1967.

Kaiper, Dan and Nan. *Tlingit, Their Art, Culture and Legends.* Vancouver: Hancock House, 1978.

Mason, Patricia F. *Indian Tales of the Northwest.* Victoria: CommCept Publishing, 1976.

Maud, Ralph. *The Salish People:* Vol. 2, *The Squamish and the Lillooet;* Vol. 4, *The Sechelt and the South-Eastern Tribes of Vancouver Island.* Vancouver: Talon Books, 1978.

Reid, Bill. *The Raven Steals the Light.* Vancouver: Douglas & McIntyre, 1984.

Reid, Martine J., PhD. *Myths and Legends of the Haida Indians of the Northwest.* Santa Barbara, Calif.: Bellerophon Books, 1987.

Seguin, Margaret. *The Tsimshian Images of the Past, Views for the Present.* Vancouver: University of British Columbia, 1984.

Smyly, John and Carolyn. *Those Born at Koona.* Vancouver: Hancock House, 1973.

Stewart, Hilary. *Looking at Indian Art of the Northwest Coast.* Vancouver: Douglas & McIntyre, 1979.

Weatherby, Hugh. *Tales the Totems Tell.* Toronto: Macmillan of Canada, 1956.

Wherry, Joseph H. *The Totem Pole Indians.* New York: Thomas Y. Crowell, 1974.

Whitaker, Pamela, as told by Wallas, Chief James. *Kwakiutl Legends.* Vancouver: Hancock House, 1981.

Further reference material:

De Armond, Dale. *Berry Woman's Children.* New York: Green Willow Books, 1985.

Foster, Scott. *Totem Talk, A Guide to Juneau Totem Poles.* Gastineau Channel Centennial Assoc., 1985.

Garner, F.R. *Haida and Tsimshian, A Photographic History.* Ottawa: National Museum of Canada.

Legends of T'Souke and West Coast Bands. Sooke Region Historical Society and Sooke (T'Souke) Band, 1978.

Postell, Alice, and Johnson, A.P. *Tlingit Legends.* The Sheldon Jackson Museum, Sitka.

Rennicke, Jeff. *Bears of Alaska, In Life and Legend.* Boulder, Colorado: Roberts Rinehart Publishers, in cooperation with Alaska Natural History Association, 1987.

Speck, Chief Henry. *Kwakiutl Art.* Vancouver, 1964.

Webber, W.L. *The Thunderbird ''Tootooch'' Legends.* Vancouver, 1952

Canadian Cataloguing in Publication Data

Coleman, Sue.
   An artist's vision

   Includes index.
   ISBN 0-9692807-4-2

   1. Coleman, Sue.   2. Indians of North America in art.   3. Animals in art.   I. Title.
   ND249.C64A4 1989   759.11   C89-091314-5

Executive Producer: Ken Budd
Designers: Sue Coleman, Alex Green, Ken Budd
Assembler: Alex Studio Ltd.
Photographer: Trevor Mills
Editor: Elaine Jones
Colour separator: Zenith Graphics Ltd.
Typesetter: VanType
Printer: Agency Press Ltd.
Binder: North-West Books Co. Ltd.

Published by:

Summer Wild
PRODUCTIONS

#2202 - 1275 Pacific Street,
Vancouver, B.C. V6E 1T6
Phone (604) 681-0015